THE LITTLE BOOK OF
Happiness

Your Guide to a Better Life

PATRICK WHYTE

D1041190

Kansas City

For my many teachers,
with heartfelt thanks.

03 BIN 10 9 8 7

ISBN: 0-7407-1031-1

Library of Congress Catalog Card Number: 00-100436

First publication by Ebury Press in Great Britain 1998

PREFACE

In my work as a psychiatrist, I have gradually come to realize that mental health is much more than the absence of mental illness. I have noticed, for example, that many people are motivated principally by anger, by resistance to unwelcome change, or by fear, the fear of some kind of a loss. Such a predisposition always risks leaving a person rather tensed up and hot, somewhat aggressive or defensive . . . often both!

Relatively few people seem to have discovered as an alternative the search for a deep and lasting happiness as the primary motivating principle in their lives. This kind of attitude tends to leave you cool, mainly, and calm.

It seems to me that everyone has a measure of choice over this.

4 *Here, then, to encourage and foster this choice is* The Little Book of Happiness, *drawn both from modern psychological theory and ancient teachings, as well as from personal experience. I am pleased to offer it with my best wishes as a starting point — perhaps a turning point — for those stepping out on this second, happier path.*

PATRICK WHITESIDE

EVERYONE WANTS TO BE HAPPY!

Everyone wants to be happy ... Think about that.

Everyone!

Be confident!

Using this book,

you are going to teach yourself
something.

Now ... Take a full breath!

If you are going to teach yourself
something,

it is best not to be in a hurry.

Be patient ... Take it slowly ...

Give yourself a proper chance.

So ...

Everyone wants to be happy.

EVERYONE!

What next?

Getting what you want makes you
happy.

10

Knowing what you want,

That's the hard part . . .

(WHAT YOU REALLY WANT IS
HAPPINESS ITSELF!)

Clear your mind . . .

And you will be happy.

Sit quietly for a while,

Undistracted . . .

Every day.

12

Be confident!

Believe in happiness . . .

You deserve it.

You don't have to make someone else
happy...

To deserve happiness for yourself.

As a matter of fact...

You cannot make anyone else happy.

14

You cannot make anyone else happy,
but you might be able to show them
how to find happiness for themselves.

Be happy and people will learn

from you.

Teach yourself to find happiness . . .

And you will set an example.

You cannot make someone else happy, but you can help them in the right direction ...

With generosity, for example.

Share your happiness!

Share your happiness ...

Give away a smile.

Give away another one.

Give away a million smiles.

Be generous!

Give away a million smiles a day.

Remember, everyone wants to be

happy.

Do not expect to feel happy all
the time.

Happiness comes and goes.

Happiness comes and goes.

Let it come . . .

Let it go.

Ask yourself as often as you like

(as often as you remember),

"Am I happy?"

If the answer is "Yes"... Enjoy the moment!

If the answer is "No," relax...

Be patient... be confident!

Happiness will surely return.

Do not trouble yourself with reasons
for happiness or unhappiness ...

It takes great skill to discover such
reasons without becoming unhappy.

Do not trouble yourself with reasons

for happiness

or unhappiness . . .

24

It takes great skill and wisdom

to discover such reasons.

You may not yet be ready . . .

Even so, be confident!

Be confident!

Be patient!

Do not trouble yourself.

Stay in the moment!

THIS IS THE BEST ADVICE

I CAN GIVE.

Stay in the moment!

Happiness can only exist in the
present . . .

In the here and the now of your life.

Happiness only exists in the present moment,

And in the very place where you are.

This is a beautiful and simple idea.

Happiness only exists in the
present moment,

When you grasp this ...

When you accept this ...

When you embrace this ...

Your life will change for the better.

28

Now, it is time to sit quietly

To reflect for a moment . . .

Undistracted.

Take a rest!

Sometimes thinking leaves us
bewildered.

Let the bewilderment pass . . .

Pause.

Take a break . . .

Let your mind work by itself.

Contentment is a calm, deep, and
more lasting form of happiness.

Teach yourself to stay right in the
moment . . .

And you will enjoy contentment.

Admittedly, this takes skill

And practice.

When the focus of your mind strays,

32

This is bewilderment . . .

The start of confusion,

Calm and happiness clouded out.

Happiness and calm go together.

When the focus of your mind strays
from the here and now...

Happiness and calm are obscured.

Human experience begins in the mind.

Human experience dwells in the mind.

What of the world outside the mind?

There is no world outside the mind.

We experience the world

with our minds.

What of the body? What of the brain?

These are at one with our minds.

So ... to be happy ...

Learn to use your mind differently.

Teach yourself how to let your mind

dwell in the present.

Teach yourself how to let your mind

dwell in each moment . . .

undistracted,

calm,

focused,

happy.

How?

To teach yourself how to let your
mind
dwell in each moment . . .

You can use your breath, or your
heartbeat, as an anchor.

Practice . . .

And you will be happy.

Sit quietly for a while,

Undistracted . . .

Every day.

Use whatever you can,

Whatever pleases you,

To bring the mind back to itself...

A pleasant sound, a tinkling bell,

A pleasant smell, perfume,

A pleasant sight, a rainbow, or

Your beloved.

Use whatever pleases you ...

A pleasant taste, the salt of sweat or
tears,

A pleasant touch, tree bark, a child's
hand.

Use your senses.

Use whatever you can . . .

A stretch, a game,

A jog, a jig,

A smile, a wave,

A hug . . .

Use your actions.

Now, again . . .

Take a rest!

44

Ask yourself, "On what does my happiness depend?"

Notice how your thoughts become troubled.

When your thoughts start to lose
focus,

When your thoughts become
troubled,

Take a rest . . .

For the moment,

Let the question go.

When you are able to reflect on the
question calmly...

Ask if your happiness seems to
depend

On the thoughts, feelings, words, or
actions

Of others.

Of course it does...

Your happiness does seem to depend
on the thoughts,

feelings, words, and actions of
others . . .

But that is an illusion.

Happiness depends . . .

On a mind that is clear.

Happiness depends on a mind that is

clear...

That is all.

That is all.

That is all!

Happiness depends on a clear
mind . . .

Like the still, reflecting surface of
a lake,

A lake on which there is no ripple
of hatred,

And not a breath of desire.

That is all . . .

50

When even worldly pleasures stir the
surface a little . . .

How much more so does anger?

Does your mind grow troubled,

reading and reflecting on this?

Why not again,

take a rest?

Let the bewilderment pass.

There is really nothing for you
to learn . . .

That your mind does not already
know.

. . . It knows how to be happy.

Like you, it wants to be happy and
calm.

This is a mystery...

Which no one need unravel.

Be confident...Be patient...

Accept the mystery.

Accept the mystery!

Simply dwell in the present
moment . . .

And be happy.

A person can have pain and stay happy...

Is this a paradox?

Is it not another mystery?

.A person can have pain and
stay happy...

56

You can have pain and stay happy.

It takes patience, admittedly,

and great skill.

Others have achieved this,

So, be confident . . .

What it takes is self-mastery . . .

This is a skill worth acquiring.

For some, even to think about pain
is to trouble the mind.

The troubled mind is an
unhappy mind . . .

So, take a rest . . .

There is no need to be in a hurry.

Take a few breaths . . .

Look around . . .

Return yourself to the present.

Take a breath . . . And another . . .

Pay attention!

Use your senses ... Seek beauty ...

60

In a flower,

A dewdrop,

In the scent of incense or woodsmoke.

Have a cup of tea.

Feel the warmth of it . . .

Taste the taste.

62

Light a candle . . .

Watch the flickering flame.

Watch the candle flame . . .

See how it changes,

Also, how it stays much the same.

Each moment it is different,

And each moment it is more or less
the same.

The same but different,

Different but the same.

The same but different,

Different but the same . . .

Many things are like this.

Understand this . . .

And you will be happy.

You will never be bored.

The same but different ... different but the same ...

People are like this ... You and me!

We are different but the same!

Understand this and you will never be bored, or frustrated, by people.

Consider your actions.

Light another candle . . .

Mindfully . . . with care . . .

Take pleasure in it.

Do everything mindfully, with care . . .

Even the chores.

Take pleasure in your actions . . .

Even those you might have wished
to avoid.

Wherever you are . . . be there!

Conscious . . . Awake!

Be present, here and now . . .

This is it!

Happiness is at hand.

But, also be *wary* of whatever seems
to give pleasure . . .

Things which bring happiness can
become pitfalls

if they become fixed as your goal . . .

Pleasure is hard to sustain.

If you get what you want,

Will you not already be fearful and
anxious of losing it?

Or will you not risk growing bored?

Take some time to reflect on all this.

Be wary, too, of successes and
winning,

For if you win . . .

Someone else has to lose . . .

And everyone wants to be happy.

Will you be happy when
another is not?

You will need great skill,
experience, serenity . . .

And the profoundest, most
joyful contentment,

Inner peace.

Even then . . .

It may not truly be possible.

How can you be happy when
another is not?

(Remember, everyone wants to
be happy.)

If you achieve deep contentment . . .

You are already a winner.

So, why conquer another?

Would there not then be . . .

Two losers?

Generosity, acceptance, tolerance,
magnanimity,
compassion, and kindness . . .

These bring happiness to the present,

And make each happy moment
seem long.

Success, fame, power, and wealth . . .

Can make a person feel good.

But is what you achieve by them
happiness?

No . . . What you achieve is only

success, fame, power, and wealth.

Success, fame, power, and wealth
can make a person feel good . . .

But, at what other person's expense?

It is easy to convince ourselves
otherwise,

Nevertheless it is true . . .

You can be poor and be happy.

You can fail, and be happy...

You can be unknown, and
be happy...

You can be without significant power,

And be happy.

To live and be happy like this takes
skill and practice...

It takes living in the present
moment...

It takes an untroubled mind...

That is all.

That is all.

That is all!

Now, I recommend it once again,

take a rest!

Take a breath.

Close your eyes.

For a moment, sit still.

Take a breath ... Keep breathing.

Sit still and close your eyes.

Sitting still, listen carefully ...

Listen to your breath in the silence.

When the mind is troubled . . .

Calm and happiness depart for
a while.

What troubles the mind?

Our emotions trouble the mind.

Anxiety, bewilderment, wanting, anger,
doubt, guilt, sorrow, and shame . . .

These emotions often trouble
the mind.

Emotions ... motion ... movement ...

Ripples on the surface of the water.

High passion ...

A storm over the lake.

When it is hard to keep the
mind still . . .

There is no need to try . . .

When the wind blows, the water
is disturbed . . .

No one is to blame.

Be confident!

If your mind is troubled,

Like water on the surface of a lake,

Be confident . . .

Be patient!

It remains ever still in the deep.

If your mind is troubled,

Like water on the surface of a lake,

It will surely settle . . .

Be patient!

Pay attention . . .

Watch your breath.

Anxiety in the mind signals threat.

What is threatening?

Usually some kind of loss.

When threatened with loss . . .

We grow anxious.

When threatened with a loss,
we have doubts

And grow confused, sometimes
angry...

We blame ourselves, feel
ashamed and guilty.

Thus...

All our emotions are linked.

People are different but the same...

the same but different!

We are especially alike in our feelings,

in our emotions.

When losses occur...

We feel sad.

Who can avoid a sense of loss?

Only those who do not want,

Who have no attachments,
no desires,

No aversions, no hatreds ...

Those with no marked likes

Or dislikes.

Who can avoid a sense of loss?

Only those deeply contented with
things just as they are.

Wishing, desire, passion, lust . . .

. . . Who is not constantly subject
to these?

These are what trouble the mind.

Wanting includes not wanting,
aversion . . .

(Which is wanting things to
be different.)

Dislike, callousness, hatred, loathing,
negative wishes, and destructive
fantasies.

These, too, are what trouble the mind.

Thus, happiness requires
constant effort . . .

And vigilance, to expose hidden
desire and self-seeking.

It demands mindfulness . . .

Presence of mind.

Let slip your vigilant guard . . .

And your mind will be troubled, again
and again . . .

By desire . . .

By passion . . .

By loathing.

But do not let this trouble

you now . . .

Take a conscious breath once

again . . . Take a rest!

Rest quietly in the present moment,

Where it is safe . . .

Safe here,

Safe now.

Let bewilderment, anxiety, anger, wanting, shame, doubt, guilt, and sorrow pass.

Bring your mind back to the present.

What brings happiness?

The absence of sorrow,

The absence of anger,

The absence of doubt,

The absence of shame.

What else brings happiness?

The absence of bewilderment,
of confusion,

The absence of anxiety, of worry,

The absence of guilt, of self-blame,

The absence of desire, of wanting.

Accept this and anger departs . . .

For anger equals resistance.

Give up your anger . . . Let it go!

Acceptance leads to serenity.

Be clear about this and confusion
settles . . .

Confusion and doubt both depart.

Clarity of mind is a great prize . . .

The key to natural wisdom.

104

So ...

Be clear, be still, and be tranquil.

Let anxiety soften, subside, and depart.

Avoid guilt, and be blameless . . .

In thought, word, and action.

Recriminations unsettle the mind.

Be patient with yourself…

Be satisfied.

Find and accept your limitations.

Thus …

Let go of self-consciousness and

Become free of your shame.

Do good . . . Earn praise . . .
Earn thanks . . .

(But take great care not to
demand them.)

Thus, as shame departs,

Self-esteem will arise . . .

Happiness is not far away.

These things are hard for some to understand,

But do not make a problem of it . . .

Relax and use effort

To keep your mind in the present.

Right here, right now . . .

Put all your energy into that.

There is no need to struggle with
desire or temptation . . .

No need to wrestle with anger.

Let them go.

Take a breath.

Count to ten.

Have a rest.

Find your way!

Find your way . . .

Find your way back . . .

Find your way back to the
present moment.

Here and now is your home.

Be forgiving, forgiving of yourself.

Tell no lies, and remember...

Leaving important things out
counts as telling a lie...

If you want to be happy,

Always tell the truth whole.

112

Wherever you are,

Sitting or standing . . .

Give up desire.

Wherever you are,

Walking or lying down . . .

Give up sorrow.

114

Wherever you are,

Lying down or standing . . .

Give up rivalry, anger, and hatred.

Wherever you are,

Walking or sitting . . .

Give up confusion and doubt.

Standing, sitting, walking, and
lying down . . .

Be calm, clear-thinking,
tranquil, accepting.

Find serenity . . . Be serene!

Sitting, standing, lying down,
and walking . . .

Be without blame,

Without fear.

Lying down, sitting, standing,
and walking . . .

Live in the moment . . . Live in joy . . .

Be happy!

The secret is . . . there's no secret!

Breathe and be mindful . . .

That is all.

Again ...

Let confusion and bewilderment

pass ...

Take a rest!

Everyone wants to be happy...

Everyone desires happiness.

This is another kind of wanting,
of desire...

It is a kind of a trap.

So ... Do not *try* to be happy!

Focus only on trying to be present ...

This is the way out of the trap.

"But this..." (I want to be happy),

"But that..." (I do not feel happy right now)...

Such thoughts only trouble the mind.

Remember...

"The key to the treasure is the
treasure."

This means the key to a joyful,
untroubled mind is a joyful,
untroubled mind.

Keep it clear...Keep it calm...

Keep it happy.

124

There can be no further wanting

Or desire for happiness . . .

If you are happy already.

Think about this if you want to . . .

But do not let yourself get confused.

Remember to take a breath . . .

Take a rest!

Perhaps you are ready to ask yourself now,

"What gets in the way of my happiness?"

Is it, "Not having what I desire?"

Is it also, and equally, "Having what I do not desire . . ."

(That is, having what you dislike . . . Having what you wish to avoid and cannot avoid)?

127

Is it one or the other of these that prevents your happiness?

It certainly seems that way, but it is
not so ...

No!

These are not what get in the way
of happiness.

It is desire and aversion themselves!

Even so, there is no need to fight
against them ...

Wanting to be rid of desire is to
double desire,

To double desire with aversion ...

Aversion is just another form of
desire.

This is another kind of trap ...

The remedy is the same ... to let go!

Let go, and return your mind to the

present ...

To this moment

Here and now.

Come on home!

Find freedom!

Dwell in the present . . .

Put all your energy into this.

"The Key to the Treasure is the
Treasure."

Your mind is the key ...

Your mind is the treasure.

If you want to be happy, never
forget this.

But, if you want to be happy,

You must forget this ...

This is a paradox ... Honor
this mystery ...

And discover what your mind
already knows.

It cannot forget, so you are free
to let go

(To let go of wanting.)

It cannot forget, so ...

You are safe ...

134

You are free!

To find happiness and to stay happy,

You need only let go of desire . . .

Especially the desire to stay happy.

Penetrate this paradox . . .

And you will know you are free.

Penetrate this paradox ...

You have only to break through
certain aspects of your conditioning.

Be confident ... Have faith!

Have faith in your treasure ...

Have faith in your mind.

Everyone wants to be happy.

If you give up trying . . .

And live in the present moment . . .

You will teach everyone how.

If you give up trying ... And live in
the present moment ...

Your happiness will teach others,

Will show everyone ...

How to be happy!

(Make everyone who is happy

your teacher.)

When faced with a mystery, take time
to admire it . . .

Sit quietly, close your eyes, take
a breath . . .

Pay attention.

The mind knows the secret.

(That there is no secret.)

140

It is not a very good secret . . .

But it is, at least, a good mystery.

Let your mind go to work on it . . .

Apply the key to the treasure.

Take a rest now, if you need one.

Reflection and rest support
one another.

Rest and reflection . . .

The passive mind working for you.

Do not tangle with the treasure ...
Admire it!

142

Follow the feelings in your mind.

Follow your senses,

Follow your thoughts,

Follow your impulses and actions.

Watch them rising and ceasing.

Follow nature . . .

Sometimes it rains,

Sometimes it shines.

Be happy with one . . .

Be happy with the other . . .

Dwell in the present.

Everything that arises, ceases . . .

Everything that is born and alive will
die and decay

(Even you . . . even me)

For some this is a barrier to happiness.

All the more reason

To dwell in the present.

Has it occurred to you that ...

A person can be happy ...

Even in the face

Of death itself?

Calling its end to mind, gives a thing
its true value . . .

146

Retaining that end in mind

Protects us against the shock, later,
of loss.

Constant mindfulness of the end of a
thing of value . . .

Of the certainty of its eventual
loss to us,

When we come to terms with this,

Helps ward off false hope and anxiety.

Apply these ideas to your life . . .

To your beloved . . . To your family . . .

To all creatures . . . To life itself . . .

It is a harsh discipline but

The rewards are great!

All that arises, ceases.

Apply this idea . . .

To our planet Earth and the Cosmos.

Then you will find wisdom . . .

Then you will find our true values.

So . . .

Have courage . . . Be confident!

Face your fears!

In the name of happiness . . .

Face your fears,

Your desires and aversions!

Face your terror, your passion, your

loathing . . .

Face them . . . and let them go!

Conquer them, and

master yourself.

In the name of happiness . . .

Have courage!

Be patient!

Be confident!

Be ever truthful, wholly truthful,
with others . . .

And with (within) yourself.

Teach yourself how to be silent . . .

How to dwell in the present moment

alone.

Learn how to discover that
this happy moment . . .

Is the eternal present.

That the sacred moment of
your birth,

Is also that of your most
hallowed death.

Teach yourself to know
incontrovertibly

And without fear that this . . .

The eternal, happy moment of
your birth,

Life and death . . .

Is your home.

Let go of fear!

Give up the desire for a long life

(Or a short one)

Give up desire!

156

Let go ... Sit still ...

Watch, listen to yourself take
a breath ...

And another ... And another ...
And another.

Live on!

Come back from anger or fear to your

true home ...

Return to the here and the now!

Simply breathe,

Simply be ...

AND ...

BE HAPPY!

Remember,

The choice is yours . . .

Make it now!